Homes

Nicola Baxter

FRANKLIN WATTS

NEW YORK • LONDON • SYDNEY

Some people live in the countryside.
Their nearest neighbours or shops
might be a long way away.

3

Some people live in a town or city.
There are many homes and shops
and places where people work nearby.

What kind of place do you live in?

There might be just one home
in a house or bungalow.
Inside a block of flats or a skyscraper,
lots of people live in separate homes.

Try this later
With your friends, paint lots of boxes
and pile them up to make a very tall building.

7

Some homes can move from place to place!

When it is cold, your home can
keep you warm.
When it is wet, your home can
keep you dry.

11

Inside a home there is somewhere to get food ready.

What are these things used for in a kitchen?

A home has places for everyone to sleep and somewhere to keep yourself clean. What other kinds of rooms do homes sometimes have?

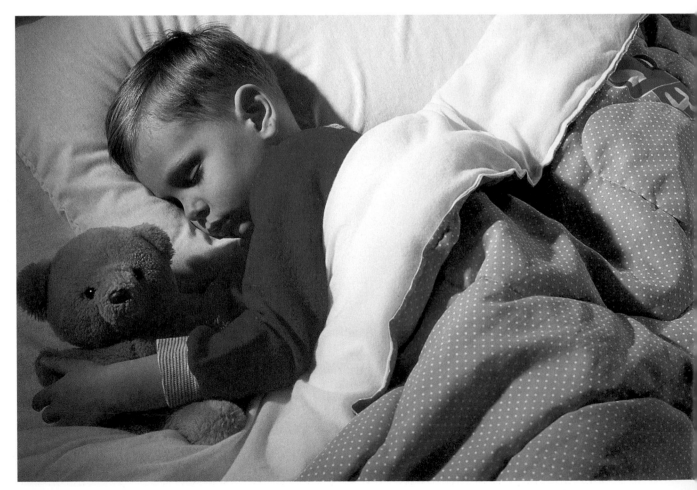

There are shelves and cupboards and drawers where all sorts of things can be kept.

If someone moves house, they often need a huge truck to carry all their things to their new home.

Home is a good place to relax with your friends and family.

Who do you spend time with in your home?

Wherever you live, home is...

where you come home to!

23

Index

© 1996 Franklin Watts
This edition 1997
Franklin Watts
96 Leonard Street
London EC2A 4RH

Franklin Watts Australia
14 Mars Road
Lane Cove, NSW 2066

Dewey Decimal Classification
Number 728
ISBN: 0 7496 2173 7

A CIP catalogue record for
this book is available from
the British Library.

Editor: Sarah Ridley

Designer: Nina Kingsbury

Illustrator: Michael Evans

The publishers would like to thank
Carol Olivier and Stephen Mabalot
of Kenmont Primary School

for their help with the cover
of this book.

Photographs: Collections 20;
James Davies Travel
Photography 5, 6, 11; Eye
Ubiquitous 8; Robert Harding
Picture Library 3; Images 12;
Peter Millard cover;
ZEFA 9, 14.

Printed in Malaysia